Prayer 101
A Practical Guide for Effective Prayer

Tamiya D. Lewis

TAMIYA D. LEWIS

Copyright © 2014 Tamiya D. Lewis

All rights reserved.

ISBN: 1466243104

TAMIYA D. LEWIS

Prayer 101
A Practical Guide for Effective Prayer

TAMIYA D. LEWIS

DEDICATION

To my loved ones that have gone on before me, I miss and love you all…

TAMIYA D. LEWIS

CONTENTS

Introduction................................12
Rebuilding a Firm Foundation 18
The Dynamics of Prayer........................24
Teach Me How to Pray..........................32
Spiritual Identity............................38
Types of Prayer...............................42
Keys to Effective Prayer......................54
Questions About Prayer........................64
Strange Fire..................................72
Tactics of Satan..............................84
What's in A Name..............................92
Conclusion................................100

TAMIYA D. LEWIS

ACKNOWLEDGEMENTS

There have been several people who have placed their stamp on my life. They range from family members to mentors, pastors, teachers and even a few friends. I am who I am today because of their influence. I've learned what I've learned because they took the time to teach me. I am truly grateful for each and every person God allowed to cross my path. To every person that assisted in my development, every individual that loved me enough to never let me settle for anything less than God's best, I extend my extreme gratitude and appreciation. I truly stand on the shoulders of GREAT men and women who have imparted a lifetime of wisdom and experiences into the fraction of time known as my life. These experiences pushed me in my last season and are catapulting me into my next season. Thank you for all you have done and I love you!

TAMIYA D. LEWIS

INTRODUCTION

What is prayer? Prayer is simply speaking or communicating with God. It is an action that is guided by the Holy Spirit. Everything that occurs in this dimension is birthed through the womb of prayer. Nations rise and fall because of prayer or the lack thereof. Laws are established or changed through prayer. Prayer allows us to speak and command Heaven's legislation and government to become law in the earth. It allows us to both, communicate with God and convey the information we receive from God to occupants in another dimension or region, such as the elements, angels, demons, principalities or powers, etcetera.

> *But He was in the stern, asleep on a pillow. And they awoke Him and said to Him, "Teacher, do You not care that we are perishing?" Then He arose and rebuked the wind, and said to the sea, "Peace, be still!" And the wind ceased and there was a great calm. (Mark 4:38, 39 NIV)*

This passage shows Jesus speaking and commanding the elements to be still or obey His command. According to the text Jesus did not just speak to God but He also spoke to the wind and the waves *(the elements)* and they in turn obeyed His words.

Prayer is a vital component in the life of every believer

and without prayer it is impossible for us to communicate with God. Through prayer some very awesome things have been done. Jesus raised Lazarus from the dead, Elijah commanded fire to fall from the sky and consume a water drenched sacrifice, Peter commanded the beggar at the gate called Beautiful to pick up his mat and walk, Joshua commanded the sun to stand still, Paul commanded a spirit of divination to leave a young girl and the list goes on.

According to the book of Genesis, power and authority was given to all of mankind.

> *...Let us make man in our likeness; let him have dominion over the fish of the sea, over the birds of the air, and over the cattle over all the earth and over every creeping thing that creeps on the earth. So God created man in His own image, in the image of God He created him; male and female. He created them. Then God blessed them and God said to them, be fruitful and multiply; fill the earth and subdue it; have dominion over the fish of the sea, over the birds of the air and over every living thing that moves on the earth. (Genesis 1:26 NIV)*

This passage deals with two specific points: the first is that all of humanity was made in God's image and the second is that mankind shall be given authority over all things on the earth. This passage does not say let us make some men or certain men in God's image but that all men are made in God's image. This passage speaks to our measure of rule.

According to this passage, total governing authority was given to mankind in the Garden of Eden. God blessed man and then commanded them to be fruitful, multiply, have dominion, fill and subdue the earth. Through this passage God was in essence saying, take care of what I have given you and have dominion over it, which is the power or right of governing and controlling. He then said nothing can enter it *(the earth)* unless you say or allow it to, and if you do allow another force to trespass into this dimension, I have given you *(man)* the ability to subdue that force or bring it under your control, to conquer and bring into subjection either by force or persuasion. This authority gives man the same rights and responsibilities given to Adam in the Garden of Eden. Powerful!

Our reign and authority are not based on the title or position we hold, but the God we serve. Just as Elijah, James, Moses and John were powerful so are we, and we have been given dominion or the authority to rule and govern the earth.

TAMIYA D. LEWIS

Lesson Overview

Key Scriptures

Mark 4:38, 39
Genesis 1:26

1. Prayer is _____ in the life of every believer, without prayer it is impossible for us to _____ with God.

2. What is prayer?

   _____

3. Examples of power displayed in prayer:

- Jesus
- Elijah
- Peter
- Paul

4. According to Genesis 1:26, what was man given?

True or False

5. ____Only some men were created in God's image and given dominion over all things.

6. ____If man allows something to enter the earth he cannot subdue that force or bring it under governmental control.

7. Nothing can enter the _____ unless man says or allows it.

8. Our reign and authority are not based on the title or position we _____, but the God we _____.

9. Just as Elijah, James, Moses and John were _____ so are we, and we have _____ been given dominion.

10. What is man's God given authority?

CHAPTER ONE
Rebuilding a Firm Foundation

Many believers struggle with prayer not because God is unwilling to respond, but because they have an inaccurate understanding of what prayer is and how it works. When the foundation is flawed, the structure built upon it becomes unstable. As a result, prayers often feel ineffective, inconsistent, or unanswered.

There are several common reasons prayer becomes hindered. Some people view prayer as a ritual reserved only for mealtimes or emergencies—something to be rushed through rather than intentionally practiced. Others refrain from praying altogether because they feel inadequate, "not holy enough," or incapable of praying the "right way." Still others only approach God in moments of crisis, seeking a quick solution rather than a sustained relationship. Regardless of the reason, these misunderstandings create distance between the believer and the power available through prayer.

To develop an effective prayer life, it is essential for the believer to have proper stewardship over their thought life. How we view **ourselves** and how we view **God** plays a critical role in whether our prayers are offered with confidence or hesitation. If faulty perceptions are left unaddressed, incorrect thought patterns begin to form. Over time, these patterns can develop into spiritual strongholds.

A **stronghold** is an emotional, mental, or spiritual fortress that restricts movement, immobilizes growth, and keeps an individual trapped in a stagnant or dying condition. Strongholds are not always obvious because they operate primarily in the mind. The battlefield of prayer is the battlefield of thought.

Scripture makes this clear:

"The weapons of our warfare are not carnal but mighty through God for the pulling down of strongholds, casting down imaginations, and every high thing that exalts itself against the knowledge of God."
— **2 Corinthians 10:4–5**

According to this passage, strongholds, vain imaginations, and lofty thoughts directly attack a believer's understanding of God. When a person's perception of God is distorted, their prayers become easily hindered. These mental structures disguise themselves as personal thoughts, convincing individuals that they are simply being realistic or self-aware. If left unchecked, the believer begins to identify with these thoughts and operate from a place of defeat rather than faith.

These thoughts often sound like:

- *God doesn't answer my prayers because He doesn't care about me.*
- *I can't pray unless I have everything together.*
- *God only hears leaders, not ordinary believers.*
- *I am insignificant.*
- *I have failed too much for God to accept me.*

The list is endless, but the source is the same—a distorted foundation.

However, Scripture declares a different reality:

> *"Now thanks be to God who always leads us in triumph in Christ, and through us diffuses the fragrance of His knowledge in every place."*
> **— 2 Corinthians 2:14**

Through Christ, we are not defeated, overlooked, or disqualified—we are victorious. Because of our relationship with Jesus, we have direct access to the Father. He is not distant or unapproachable. He is our Savior, our Lord, our Advocate, and our closest friend.

Rebuilding a firm foundation begins with renewing the mind, uprooting false beliefs, and embracing the truth of who God is and who we are in Him. When the foundation is restored, prayer becomes effective, confident, and powerful.

TAMIYA D. LEWIS

Lesson Overview

I Corinthians 10:4, 5
John 14:12-14
Jeremiah 22:2, 3

1. What is a stronghold?
   _____

2. Where do strongholds attack?
   _____

3. What is the mistake most new believers make?

   _____

4. How important is a person's belief structure when attempting to enter into prayer?

   _____

True or False

5. _____ God doesn't answer my prayers because He doesn't really care about me.

6. _____ I can't pray if I am not right.

7. _____ God only hears the leadership, He doesn't hear me.

8. What are some of the strongholds or untruths that you have allowed to hinder your prayers?
   _____

9. What will you do different to stop this stronghold from hindering you?

CHAPTER TWO
The Dynamics of Prayer

There are three important dynamics involved in prayer; they are formula, focus and stance. Formula emphasizes the equation necessary in order to communicate with God effectively, focus allows individuals to direct their energy toward a target and stance deals with the leverage applied while in prayer.

Just as there is a formula or recipe that shows you how to bake a cake, there is also a formula that shows you how to pray. The formula is simple: it is read, pray, ask, believe, expect and receive.

- Read God's Word. The answer to any problem we face can be found in the Word of God.

    Joshua 1: 8 This book of the law (bible) *shall not depart from your mouth but you shall meditate on it day and night that you may observe to do according to all that is written in it. For then you will make your way prosperous, and then you will have good success.*

    The foundation for prayer is found in the Word of God. All the promises of God are found in His Word.

Pray the Word according to your situation. God esteems His Word very highly and is only moved by His Word:
I will worship toward thy holy temple and give thanks unto thy name for thy loving kindness and for thy truth. For thou has magnified thy word above all thy name.

(Psalms 157:2 NIV)

- Ask God to perform any function according to what you have read in His Word.

I John 5:14, 15 *Now this is the confidence that we have in Him, that if we ask anything according to His will. He hears us and if we know that He hears us whatever we ask, we know that we have the petitions that we asked of Him.*

- Believe in faith that you have received what you have asked for.

Mark 9:23 Jesus said to him, if you can believe, all things are possible.

- Receive the answer.

Mark 11:24 Therefore I tell you, whatever you ask for in prayer, believe that you have received it, and it will be yours.

The next dynamic is focus. There are three

reasons why focus is important. First, focus teaches individuals precision and allows them to set their sight towards an attainable target. *Precision is the ability of a measurement to be consistently reproduced.* According to this definition, precision is developed by careful repetition and purposeful practice. No one who desires to ride a bike quits the first time they fall off. They instead get up, dusts themselves off and continues to try until they master riding without falling. Just as one goes through this process while attempting to ride a bike, one should keep this same mindset while attempting to communicate with God. The first time an individual prays both publicly and privately, it feels awkward but remain consistent. The more time you spend with God, seeking His face, the easier it becomes.

The second point is that, focused prayers are accurate prayers. If one is not praying focused prayers they are praying what I like to refer to as an "anything tactic", which involves the individual praying on a whim. People that do this, approach prayer like a free-for-all. They pray whatever comes to mind, whenever they decide to pray. In order to measure your accuracy you must have a list or a goal. If there is no goal how will you know if you have achieved anything? It's simple, you will not. If you are sick and desire to be healed you don't need to waste your time praying that God will correct global warming. You need to focus your prayers toward healing. Praying without a focus limits the accuracy of your prayers and causes you to both hit and miss your designated target.

Applying proper boundaries are important when engaging in prayer.

If one is praying without a focus they are releasing misguided words, with no strategic direction. If not careful this kind of praying can lead an individual to praying witchcraft prayers.

When many people think of witchcraft they think of someone standing over a cauldron with a large wooden spoon speaking damning words and throwing things into a brewing pot. This is an extreme form of witchcraft.

Praying anything contrary to God's Word is witchcraft. That is why it is important for every believer to read the Word of God and get a foundational base for the prayers that are prayed.

Lastly there is stance. *Stance is a mental or emotional position adopted with respect to something.* In prayer stance is important because every situation we face is not the same, there are times that you will receive an immediate answer to prayers that are prayed, (i.e. healing manifested immediately) and then there will be times that you will have to contend in prayer and hold on to your faith confession. (by faith I am healed even though I don't see the manifestation of healing in my body) It is important to note that the enemy does not have authority over us, the bible says that he is a roaring lion seeking who he may devour. The reason roaring is emphasized is because he hurls loud accusations, and threats in an attempt to wear us down and talk us out of our God given blessing, rights and authority. As a result, it is important that we maintain an aggressive stance in prayer stand on God's promises with all diligence because He is faithful to honor His word and is a rewarder of them that diligently seek Him.

Lesson Overview

Key Scriptures

1 John 5:14, 15
Isaiah 53:5
Joshua 1: 8
Psalms 157:2
I John 5:14, 15
Mark 9:23
Mark 11

1. What are three dynamics of prayer?

   _____

   _____

2. _____ is needed to receive an answer to our prayers.

3. What is the formula involved with prayer?

   _____

4. Praying anything_____ the accuracy of your prayers and causes you to both _____ and _____ your _____ target.

5. What is focus?

6. Why is focus important?

7. Prayer without a focus is _____, because there is no ground or root for prayer or the words released to stand on.

8. Praying without a focus is simply releasing _____ words with no strategic direction.

9. What is stance?

10. Why is it important that every believer have a stance while in prayer?

TAMIYA D. LEWIS

CHAPTER THREE
Teach Me How to Pray

One day Jesus was praying in a certain place. When He finished, one of His disciples said to Him, "Lord, teach us to pray, just as John taught his disciples." He said to them, "When you pray, say: " Father, hallowed be your name, your kingdom come. Give us each day our daily bread. Forgive us our sins, for we also forgive everyone who sins against us. And lead us not into temptation. (Luke 11:1-4 NIV)

Jesus was a man of prayer. Prayer was not an occasional discipline for Him—it was a lifestyle. He prayed early in the morning, late at night, in solitude, and in the presence of others. His prayers produced undeniable results: authority over demons, miraculous provision, healing for the sick, wisdom for leadership, and intimate communion with the Father.

In Luke 11, the disciples overhear Jesus praying and are deeply moved. One of them finally asks a powerful question: *"Lord, teach us to pray."* This request is significant because the disciples were not strangers to prayer. Many of them were Jews who had been taught from childhood how to read Scripture, recite prayers, and follow religious traditions. Prayer was familiar to them.

Yet after observing Jesus, they realized something crucial—their prayers lacked the power, intimacy, and effectiveness that His prayers carried. They watched signs, wonders, and miracles flow from His communion with God and recognized that prayer, as Jesus practiced it, was different. What they had learned was no longer sufficient for what they were witnessing. They wanted access to the same spiritual authority and results.

When Jesus responded, He did not give them a prayer to memorize merely as a religious ritual. For generations, many Christians have been taught to quote what is commonly called *The Lord's Prayer* word for word. While there is nothing wrong with praying it verbatim, it is essential to understand that Jesus was not instructing His disciples to repeat His exact words mechanically. Instead, He was teaching them a **pattern**, a **framework**, and **guiding principles** for effective prayer.

The Lord's Prayer is a model that reveals how to approach God, how to align with His will, and how to live dependently and righteously before Him. Each component teaches us something vital about our relationship with the Father.

The Pattern of Prayer Jesus Taught

A. Address God Personally — *"Father"*
Prayer begins with relationship. Jesus teaches us to

approach God not as a distant deity, but as a loving Father. This establishes intimacy, trust, and identity. We pray not as strangers, but as children who belong to Him.

B. Reverence God for Who He Is — *"Hallowed be your name"*
Before making requests, we honor God. To "hallow" His name means to recognize His holiness, greatness, and worthiness. Worship aligns our hearts with heaven and reminds us who God is.

C. Align with God's Will — *"Your kingdom come"*
Prayer is not about bending God's will to match ours, but aligning ourselves with His purposes. When we pray for His kingdom to come, we are inviting His rule, authority, and righteousness to manifest in the earth through our lives.

D. Depend on God for Daily Provision — *"Give us each day our daily bread"*
Jesus teaches us daily dependence. God cares about both spiritual and practical needs. This request acknowledges that everything we need—strength, wisdom, provision, and sustenance—comes from Him.

E. Practice Forgiveness and Repentance — *"Forgive us our sins, for we also forgive everyone who sins against us"*
Effective prayer requires a clean heart. We must

continually ask God to forgive us while also choosing to forgive others. Unforgiveness hinders intimacy with God and blocks spiritual flow.

F. Seek God's Guidance and Protection — *"Lead us not into temptation"*
This is a prayer for direction, discernment, and deliverance. We ask God to guide our steps, guard our hearts, and keep us from paths that lead to spiritual compromise and harm.

Through this model, Jesus teaches us that prayer is not merely words spoken—it is a posture of the heart. When we pray according to this pattern, we grow in intimacy with God, align with His will, and walk in greater spiritual authority and effectiveness.

PRAYER 101

Lesson Overview

Key Scriptures

Luke 11:1-4
Matthew 6:19

1. Jesus did not intend for the _____ to pray the exact prayer given in Mathew 6:19 but He was instead giving them a _____ prayer.

2. _____ God personally (our Father)

3. Reverence God for _____ He is (Hallowed be your name)

4. Allow God to _____ His will in the earth (Your kingdom come, your will be done)

5. _____ God to _____ for your every need (Give us this day our daily bread)

6. Both _____ others for the sins they commit against you and ask God to forgive you for the sins you _____ (forgive us our debts as we forgive our debtors)

35

7. Ask for _____ in your everyday life (lead us not into temptation but deliver us from evil)

CHAPTER FOUR
Spiritual Identity

But you are a chosen generation, a royal priesthood, a holy nation, a people for a possession so that you might speak of the praises of Him who has called you out of darkness into His marvelous light. (I Peter 2:9 NIV)

Understanding spiritual identity is foundational to living an effective Christian life. Scripture declares that God's people are not ordinary—we are chosen, royal, holy, and set apart for divine purpose. Our identity is not defined by culture, circumstance, or past failures, but by God's sovereign design and redemptive work.

From the beginning, God created humanity to rule and steward the earth while proclaiming His glory. When God established the heavens and the earth, it was already understood that He alone is the Supreme Ruler and Creator. Yet, in His wisdom, God chose to create a masterpiece that reflected His own nature—mankind. Scripture records God saying, *"Let Us make man in Our image, according to Our likeness"* (Genesis 1:26).

Being created in God's image and likeness means we were designed to function with authority, responsibility, and purpose. Humanity was originally commissioned to rule, govern, and steward creation under God's dominion. This royal assignment reveals that from the beginning, mankind carried a kingly identity.

However, through sin, humanity lost its rightful authority and fellowship with God. What was intended to be exercised in righteousness was surrendered through disobedience. Yet God, rich in mercy, sent His Son, Jesus Christ, to restore what was lost. Through His death, burial, and resurrection, Jesus redeemed us, reestablished our relationship with the Father, and restored our spiritual authority. As a result, believers are not only children of God—we are heirs and kings under His lordship.

Genesis 1 reveals that God created the universe by the power of His spoken word. He did not shape creation with His hands; instead, He spoke, and all things came into existence. The King of Kings used words to bring order, form, and life. As His children, we have been given the capacity to speak in alignment with His Word and authority—not independently of Him, but in submission to His will.

Kings do not beg; they decree. They speak with authority because of their position. Likewise, when believers speak God's Word in faith, heaven and earth respond in the spiritual realm. Our authority is not rooted in personal power, but in our identity in Christ and agreement with God's Word. As Dr. Cindy Trimm wisely states, *"Words have presence. Words have power. Words have prophetic implications with no geographical limitations."* Words, when aligned with God's truth, are a powerful spiritual resource capable of shifting circumstances and environments.

Scripture further affirms our position in Christ:

"Let us then approach God's throne of grace with confidence, so that we may receive mercy and find grace to help us in our time of need."
— **Hebrews 4:16 (NIV)**

Through Christ, we hold both an inherited position and a redeemed position with God. We inherit identity through creation, and we are redeemed through the finished work of Jesus Christ. This restored identity gives us bold access to God's presence, confidence in prayer, and authority to live out our calling as a royal priesthood—declaring His praises and advancing His kingdom in the earth.

When believers fully understand who they are in Christ, they no longer live beneath their privilege. Instead, they walk in confidence, authority, and purpose, shining as those who have been called out of darkness into His marvelous light.

Lesson Overview

Key Scriptures

1 Peter 2:9
Genesis 2
Hebrews 4:16

1. What did God create his people to do?
   _____

2. Whose image was mankind made in?
   _____

3. How did God form the earth?
   _____

Fill in the blank

_____ have presence, words have _____, words have _____ implications with no geographical _____."

5. What is our prayer position?
   _____

6. Are we supposed to beg in prayer?

   _____

7. The position that we have is _____?

CHAPTER FIVE
Types of Prayer

Just as there are many ways to communicate with one another, there are also multiple ways to communicate with God through prayer. Prayer is not limited to one expression or formula; rather, it allows us to speak to God according to the specific situation, need, or season we are facing.

The Apostle Paul makes this clear when he writes:

> *"First of all, then, I urge that supplications, prayers, intercessions, and thanksgivings be made for all people."*
> **— 1 Timothy 2:1 (NIV)**

In this passage, Paul instructs Timothy to engage in different types of prayer to effectively meet the needs of God's people. Understanding **what type of prayer to pray—and when to pray it—is vital to our spiritual growth, emotional health, and effectiveness as believers**.

Below are several biblical categories of prayer that every Christian should understand and practice.

A. Thanksgiving

Thanksgiving is the expression of gratitude for what God has already done. It shifts our focus from lack to abundance and reminds us of God's faithfulness.

> *"Give thanks in all circumstances; for this is God's will for you in Christ Jesus."*
> — **1 Thessalonians 5:18 (NIV)**
> *"Do not be anxious about anything... with thanksgiving, present your requests to God."*
> — **Philippians 4:6 (NIV)**

B. Petition

Petition is a respectful and humble request made to a superior authority. It involves bringing personal needs before God with reverence and submission.

> *"During the days of Jesus' life on earth, He offered up prayers and petitions with loud cries and tears to the One who could save Him from death, and He was heard because of His reverent submission."*
> — **Hebrews 5:7–8 (NIV)**

Even Jesus modeled petition, demonstrating that asking God is not weakness—it is trust.

C. Confession

Confession is the honest acknowledgment of sin, weakness, or wrongdoing. It restores fellowship with God and opens the door to healing.

"Therefore confess your sins to each other and pray for each other so that you may be healed. The prayer of a righteous person is powerful and effective."
— **James 5:16 (NIV)**

D. Intercession

Intercession is standing in the gap on behalf of others—praying for people, communities, or nations as if their burden were your own.

Nehemiah provides a powerful example of intercession in **Nehemiah 1:1–11**, where he weeps, fasts, confesses corporate sin, and pleads with God for the restoration of Jerusalem. His prayer demonstrates compassion, repentance, and bold faith.

E. Praise

Praise is the expression of admiration, approval, and honor toward God. It magnifies God's greatness and lifts our hearts above circumstances.

"Because Your lovingkindness is better than life, my lips shall praise You... My mouth shall praise You with joyful lips."
— **Psalm 63:3–5 (NKJV)**

F. Supplication

Supplication is earnest and humble pleading before God. It often accompanies times of urgency or deep need.

> *"Do not be anxious about anything, but in everything, by prayer and supplication, with thanksgiving, present your requests to God."*
> — **Philippians 4:6 (NIV)**

G. Worship

Worship focuses on **who God is**, not merely what He does. Both praise and worship express honor, but worship is deeper—it is adoration, surrender, and reverence.

"Yet a time is coming and has now come when the true worshipers will worship the Father in spirit and in truth."
— **John 4:23–24 (NIV)**

"LORD, there is no one like You to help the powerless against the mighty."
— **2 Chronicles 14:11 (NIV)**

H. Praying in Tongues

Praying in tongues is a spiritual gift that allows believers to communicate directly with God spirit-to-spirit. It strengthens the inner person and assists when words fail.

Benefits include:

- Speaking directly to God
- Spiritual edification
- Praying beyond human understanding

"For anyone who speaks in a tongue does not speak to people but to God."
— **1 Corinthians 14:2 (NIV)**
"Build yourselves up in your most holy faith and pray

in the Holy Spirit."
— **Jude 20 (NIV)**
"The Spirit Himself intercedes for us with groanings too deep for words."
— **Romans 8:26–27 (NIV)**

I. Prayer of Agreement

The prayer of agreement involves believers coming into spiritual harmony, trusting God together for a shared outcome.

"If two of you on earth agree about anything they ask for, it will be done for them by my Father in heaven."
— **Matthew 18:19–20 (NIV)**

J. Prayer of Faith

Faith-filled prayer is steadfast belief in God's power and promises. It trusts God completely, regardless of visible circumstances.

"The prayer offered in faith will make the sick person well."
— **James 5:15 (NIV)**

James highlights Elijah as an example, reminding us that effective prayer is not reserved for spiritual elites—*Elijah was a man just like us.*

K. Spiritual Warfare

Spiritual warfare prayer confronts opposition in the spiritual realm using God-given authority and spiritual weapons.

"The weapons of our warfare are not of this world, but mighty through God for the pulling down of strongholds."
— 2 Corinthians 10:3–5 (NKJV)

Listening as Part of Prayer

Prayer is not meant to be a one-sided conversation. While speaking to God is essential, we must also create space to **listen**. If prayer consists only of asking without acknowledging, thanking, or hearing from God, the relationship becomes transactional rather than relational.

True prayer flows from intimacy—not merely the desire for God's blessings, but from the joy of knowing Him.

When believers learn to pray in multiple dimensions, they grow in spiritual maturity, discernment, and depth—developing a vibrant, balanced, and powerful prayer life.

Lesson Overview

Key Scriptures

Philippians 4:6
1 Thessalonians 5:18
Hebrews 5:7, 8
Philippians 4:6
James 5:16
Nehemiah 1-11
II Kings 19:15-17
II Chronicles 14:11
John 4:21-24
I Corinthians 14:2
Jude 20
Matthew 18:18-20
Psalms 63:3-5
Romans 8:26, 27
James 5:13-19
II Corinthians 10:3-5

True or False

1. _____All communication is not the same.

2. _____There is only one type of prayer.

Matching Exercise

3. ____Agreement

4. ____Spiritual Warfare

5. ____Petition

6. ____Thanksgiving

7. ____Tongues

8. ____Supplication

9. ____Praise

10. ____Intercession

11. ____Confession

12. ____Worship

13. ____Faith

PRAYER 101

(A) A solemn supplication or request to a superior authority.

(B) Your expressed appreciation for what God has done for you.

(C) Avowal; admission; acknowledgement; a confession of incompetence; an admission of misdeeds or faults.

(D) Standing in the gap for another or stand in someone else's place.

(E) Expression of approval, commendation or admiration.

(F) To ask for humbly or earnestly, as by praying. To make humble entreaty to; beseech.

G) Thanking or praising God for who He is, not what He can do.

(H) Spirit to spirit communication with God.

(I) Steadfast belief.

(J) Harmony of opinions, actions of characters.

(K) The art of warring in the realm of the spirit.

CHAPTER SIX
Keys to Effective Prayer

If you then being evil know how to give good gifts to your children, how much more will your Father who is in heaven give good things to those who ask. (Matthew 7:11 NIV)

Effective prayer is not accidental—it is intentional. God desires His children to pray with confidence, understanding, and authority. Throughout Scripture, we see that God wants His people to know the rights, privileges, and responsibilities that come with being heirs of His kingdom. As believers, we are heirs of God and joint heirs with Christ. This inheritance gives us access, authority, and expectation in prayer.

God does not want His children approaching Him timidly or ignorantly. He invites us to pray with assurance, knowing that He is a good Father who delights in responding to His children. Below are several essential keys every believer must understand in order to engage God effectively in prayer.

A. Know Who You Are

Effective prayer begins with identity. If you do not know who you are, you will struggle to pray with confidence.

"Because you are sons, God sent the Spirit of His Son into our hearts, the Spirit who calls out, 'Abba, Father.' So you are no longer a slave, but a son; and since you are a son, God has made you also an heir."
— **Galatians 4:6–7 (NIV)**

When you understand that you are a son or daughter—not a servant trying to earn favor—you pray from relationship, not fear.

B. Know God's Word

Prayer without knowledge of Scripture is dangerous. The Word of God establishes boundaries, authority, and confidence in prayer. When you know what God has already spoken, you know how to pray in alignment with His will.

> *"Do not let this Book of the Law depart from your mouth; meditate on it day and night... Then you will be prosperous and successful."*
> — **Joshua 1:8 (NIV)**

The stronger your foundation in the Word, the stronger your prayer life will be.

C. Know Your Position

Many believers waste time engaging in unnecessary "word wars" with the enemy. Jesus did not debate Satan—He declared truth and stayed focused on His assignment.

In **Matthew 4:1–11**, Jesus responds to every temptation with *"It is written."* He neither argued nor entertained distractions. Once His authority was established, Satan left.

Word wars are distractions designed to pull believers off mission. Authority does not need to shout—it speaks with certainty.

D. Know Your Measure of Rule

The incident involving the sons of Sceva teaches a powerful lesson:

"Jesus I know, and Paul I know about, but who are you?"
— **Acts 19:15 (NIV)**

These men attempted to operate in authority they did not possess. They relied on someone else's relationship with God rather than cultivating their own. Authority flows from intimacy, obedience, and spiritual maturity—not imitation.

Every believer must know their spiritual jurisdiction and never attempt to operate beyond it.

E. Know God's Will

Confidence in prayer comes from alignment with God's will.

"If we ask anything according to His will, He hears us."
— 1 John 5:14 (NIV)

The Word of God reveals the will of God. When you pray according to Scripture, you pray with assurance.

F. Ask God Boldly

God knows your needs—but He still requires you to ask.

"Ask and it will be given to you; seek and you will find; knock and the door will be opened."
— **Matthew 7:7 (NIV)**

Asking is an act of faith and dependence, not weakness.

G. Believe God Will Answer

Faith is essential to effective prayer.

"Whatever you ask in prayer, believing, you will receive."
— **Matthew 21:22 (NKJV)**

Jesus taught His disciples that faith-filled prayer carries authority. Doubt neutralizes expectation, but faith activates results.

H. Maintain Faith When the Answer Is Delayed

Not every prayer is answered immediately. Delay does not mean denial. Many biblical figures waited years for God's promises to manifest.

Hebrews 11 reminds us that Noah, Abraham, and others lived by faith long before they saw fulfillment. Their faith sustained them through waiting.

Faith is trusting God even when silence seems loud.

I. Understand God as Your Father

Jesus made a way for believers to approach the Father directly.

"Whatever you ask the Father in My name, He will give you… Ask and you will receive, that your joy may be full."
— **John 16:23–24 (NKJV)**

Prayer is not about convincing God—it is about communing with a loving Father who has already made provision.

Closing Thought

Effective prayer flows from identity, alignment, faith, and relationship. When believers understand who they are, know God's Word, walk in authority, and trust

God's timing, prayer becomes powerful, confident, and productive. Prayer is not merely a spiritual discipline—it is a kingdom privilege.

Lesson Overview

Key Scriptures
Galatians 4:4-7
Joshua 1:8
Acts 19:13-16
I John 5:14, 15
Matthew 7:11
Matthew 21:18-22
Hebrews 11:1-12
John 16:23, 24
Romans 8:17

True or False

1. ___We are children of God, and heirs to His promises.

2.___We should not expect God to bless us.

3. One must _____ the privileges, promises and restrictions _____ in God's Word for themselves

4.Name 7 of the nine keys to executing prayer.
1. _____

2. _____

3. _____

4. _____

5. _____

6. _____

7. _____

PRAYER 101

CHAPTER SEVEN
Questions About Prayer

This chapter addresses several common questions believers often have about prayer. Many Christians desire to pray effectively but struggle with doubt, confusion, or unmet expectations. Scripture provides clarity, reassurance, and direction for each of these concerns.

A. What Do You Do When Your Prayers Don't Seem to Be Answered?

The simple answer is: **keep praying**.

Jesus addressed this very issue when He taught His disciples about persistence in prayer.

"Then Jesus told His disciples a parable to show them that they should always pray and not give up."
— **Luke 18:1 (NIV)**

In the parable of the persistent widow (Luke 18:1–8), Jesus illustrates that continual prayer demonstrates faith and perseverance. God is not like the unjust judge—He is loving and attentive—but persistence keeps us aligned with God rather than growing discouraged.

Believers must also recognize that we have a real spiritual enemy who seeks to hinder answers and disrupt our agreement with God. Persistence in prayer keeps us spiritually positioned until the answer manifests.

B. Why Does It Seem Like God Only Hears Those in Leadership?

God does **not** limit His attention to leaders. He hears all who come to Him through Christ.

"If you ask anything in My name, I will do it."
— **John 14:14 (NKJV)**

Every believer has direct access to God because of their relationship with Jesus. Through Christ, God is approachable, personal, and relational—not distant or exclusive.

"Call to Me, and I will answer you and show you great and mighty things."
— **Jeremiah 33:3 (NIV)**
"If you abide in Me, and My words abide in you, you will ask what you desire, and it shall be done for you."
— **John 15:7 (NIV)**

Leadership does not grant special access—relationship does.

C. How Do I Develop Intimacy with Someone I Don't Fully Understand?

Intimacy is built through **communication**, not complete understanding. Intimacy grows as we spend time with God, speak with Him, and listen to Him.

Prayer is dialogue, not monologue. As we communicate with God, intimacy is formed naturally.

"God is Spirit, and those who worship Him must worship in spirit and truth."
— **John 4:23–24 (NIV)**

You do not need to understand everything about God to be close to Him—you need to pursue Him.

D. Why Are Some Prayers Answered While Others Seem Unanswered?

Prayer always generates a response—but the response may not always align with our expectations or timing.

Daniel's prayer in **Daniel 10:12–14** reveals that answers can be delayed due to spiritual resistance. Sometimes the answer is **yes**, sometimes **no**, and sometimes **not yet**.

God operates according to His divine timetable. Delay is often preparation, protection, or positioning.

E. What If I Don't Know How to Pray?

God has already made provision for this through the Holy Spirit.

"The Spirit helps us in our weakness… the Spirit Himself intercedes for us."
— **Romans 8:26–27 (NLT)**

When words fail, the Holy Spirit steps in. You are never praying alone.

F. Why Should I Pray?

Prayer develops relationship. It deepens intimacy and keeps communication open between us and God.

Prayer is not only about speaking—it is also about listening. One-sided communication is unhealthy in any relationship.

"They will call on My name, and I will answer them... 'The LORD is our God.'"
— **Zechariah 13:9 (NLT)**

Prayer keeps the relationship alive and active.

G. Is There a Correct Physical Position for Prayer?

There is no single posture required for prayer. Scripture shows people praying in many ways:

- Kneeling (1 Kings 8:54)
- Bowing (Exodus 4:31)
- Lying face down (Matthew 26:39)
- Standing (1 Kings 8:22)

You may pray silently or aloud, with eyes open or closed. What matters is the posture of the heart, not the position of the body.

H. Are There Specific Words I Should Use When Praying?

Prayer is simply communication with your Father. God is not impressed by eloquence or repetition—He is moved by sincerity and faith.

"When you pray, don't babble on and on… They think their prayers are answered merely by repeating their words again and again."
— **Matthew 6:7 (NLT)**

Speak to God naturally, honestly, and authentically. Talk to Him as you would a trusted friend—because in Christ, He is exactly that.

Closing Thought

Prayer is not about perfection—it is about connection. When believers understand prayer as relationship rather than ritual, it becomes a source of strength, clarity, and peace.

Lesson Overview

Key Scriptures
Matt 7:7
Luke 18:1-8
Daniel 10:2, 3, 10-14
John 14:12-14
Jeremiah 33:2, 3
John 15:7
John 4:23, 24
Romans 8:26-27
Zechariah 13:9
1 Kings 8:45
Exodus 4:31
2 Chronicles 20:18
Matthew 26:39
1 Kings 8:22
Matthew 6:7

1. Why should I pray?

   _____

What do you do if your prayers don't seem to be answered?

   _____

3. What scriptures support this statement?

   _____

   What is intimacy?

PRAYER 101

4. Why does it seem like my prayers are hitting a ceiling?
_____

True or False

5.___You have to use big words while praying.

6.___ There is no correct posture or position in prayer.

Multiple Choice

(Circle the answer that best supports the question.)

7. God only hears the leadership, and doesn't hear me.
   (A) Jn 14:12-14
   (B) Jer. 33:2, 3
   (C) Luke 18:1-8
   (D) None of the above

8. What do you do when your prayers don't seem to be answered?

(A) Daniel 10:2,3
(B) Ps 1:1
(C) Nothing
(D) None of the above

CHAPTER EIGHT
Strange Fire

And Nadab and Abihu, the sons of Aaron, took either of them his censer, and put fire therein, and put incense thereon, and offered strange fire before the LORD, which Hing of getting commanded them not. And there went out fire from the LORD, and devoured them, and they died before the LORD. Then Moses said unto Aaron, This is it that the LORD spake, saying, I will be sanctified in them that come nigh me, and before all the people I will be glorified. And Aaron held his peace. (Leviticus 10:1-3 NIV)

The account of Nadab and Abihu is one of the most sobering warnings in Scripture regarding how God must be approached. These men entered the presence of the Lord and offered **unauthorized (strange) fire**— a sacrifice God had neither commanded nor approved.

For any sacrifice to be acceptable to God, **two requirements must be met**:

1. The sacrifice must be **sanctioned by God**
2. The sacrifice must be offered in **proper order**

Nadab and Abihu violated both.

According to Jewish law and priestly order, the offering they attempted was reserved **exclusively for the High Priest**. Even the High Priest could not enter the Holy of Holies without undergoing strict sanctification and consecration. Failure to do so resulted in immediate death. Nadab and Abihu disregarded divine order, authority, and holiness—and the consequence was fatal.

Strange Fire Today

A common response is: *"That was Old Testament. How does this apply today?"*

The answer is simple: **strange fire still exists**, but it manifests differently.

Today, strange fire is offered when believers attempt to approach God **while ignoring issues of the heart**, unrepented sin, or disobedience. Prayer offered from an unclean heart creates spiritual interference—it is communication out of alignment.

"Above all else, guard your heart, for everything you do flows from it."
— **Proverbs 4:23 (NIV)**

An unguarded heart restricts spiritual access and can become the greatest hindrance to answered prayer.

The Deceptive Nature of the Heart

Scripture warns that the heart can be dangerously misleading:

"The heart is deceitful above all things and beyond cure. Who can understand it?"
— **Jeremiah 17:9 (KJV)**

A believer may sincerely think everything is fine while hidden issues quietly contaminate their spiritual life. This is why prayer must be accompanied by self-examination and repentance.

Prayer is sacred communication. Attempting to commune with a holy God while harboring sin produces separation.

Who May Enter God's Presence?

"Who may ascend the mountain of the LORD?
Who may stand in His holy place?
The one who has clean hands and a pure heart."
— **Psalm 24:3–4 (NIV)**

Purity of heart is not optional—it is foundational. God is holy, and His presence must never be approached casually or irreverently.

David understood this deeply:

"Create in me a clean heart, O God, and renew a right spirit within me."
— **Psalm 51:10 (NKJV)**

Prayer Blockers: Modern Strange Fire

Unaddressed heart issues act like **gatekeepers**, stopping prayers from reaching fruition. Below are some of the most common spiritual blockages:

A. Unforgiveness

Unforgiveness poisons prayer and invites torment.

"This is how my heavenly Father will treat each of you unless you forgive your brother from your heart."
— **Matthew 18:35 (NIV)**

B. Hidden Sin

Lucifer fell not because of open rebellion, but hidden iniquity.

"You were blameless… till wickedness was found in you."
— **Ezekiel 28:15 (NIV)**

Hidden sin eventually exposes itself.

C. Non-Repentance

God gives space to repent—but refusal invites judgment.

"I have given her time to repent… but she is unwilling."
— **Revelation 2:21 (NIV)**

D. A Corrupt Mindset

"Do not conform to the pattern of this world, but be transformed by the renewing of your mind."
— **Romans 12:2 (NIV)**

Your mindset determines your spiritual clarity.

E. Unbelief

"They were not able to enter, because of their unbelief."
— **Hebrews 3:19 (NIV)**

Unbelief hardens the heart and limits God's work.

F. Disobedience

"Then they will call to me but I will not answer."
— **Proverbs 1:28 (NIV)**

Delayed obedience is still disobedience.

G. Cherished (Secret) Sin

"If I had cherished sin in my heart, the Lord would not have listened."
— **Psalm 66:18 (NIV)**

H. Indifference

"Because you are lukewarm… I am about to spit you out of my mouth."
— **Revelation 3:16 (NIV)**

I. Neglect of Mercy

"Whoever shuts their ears to the cry of the poor will also cry out and not be answered."
— **Proverbs 21:13 (NIV)**

J. Despising God's Instruction

"If anyone turns a deaf ear to my instruction, even their prayers are detestable."
— **Proverbs 28:9 (NIV)**

K. Blood Guilt

"Your hands are full of blood!"
— **Isaiah 1:15 (NIV)**

L. Iniquity

"Your iniquities have separated you from your God."
— **Isaiah 59:2 (NIV)**

M. Stubbornness

"I will break down your stubborn pride."
— **Leviticus 26:19 (NIV)**

N. Doubt

"That person should not expect to receive anything from the Lord."
— **James 1:7 (NIV)**

O. Self-Indulgence

"You ask with wrong motives."
— **James 4:3 (NIV)**

P. Instability

"Beguiling unstable souls."
— **2 Peter 2:14 (KJV)**

The Antidote to Strange Fire

The solution is not complicated—but it is intentional.

1. Forgive

Forgiveness clears spiritual pathways.

"When you stand praying, if you hold anything against anyone, forgive them."
— **Mark 11:25 (NIV)**

---

2. Repent

Repentance means changing your mind and direction. It restores access and intimacy.

"As far as the east is from the west, so far has He removed our transgressions from us."
— **Psalm 103:12 (NIV)**

Final Exhortation

Strange fire is not about perfection—it is about **alignment**. God is holy, merciful, and compassionate, but He will not compromise His holiness.

When believers guard their hearts, forgive freely, and walk in repentance, prayer becomes pure, powerful, and unhindered.

"Let us lay aside every weight, and the sin which so easily ensnares us."
— **Hebrews 12:1 (NKJV)**

Holiness does not repel God's presence—it **invites** it.

Lesson Overview

Key Scriptures
Matthew 18:21-35
Matthew 6:14, 15
Ezekiel 28:14, 15
Luke 18:1-8
Daniel 10:2, 3, 10-14
Matt 7:7
John 15:7, 8
Jeremiah 33:2, 3
John 14:12-14
Hebrews 3:12-19
Romans 12:2
Proverbs 12:8
Revelation 2:18-22

1. What two functions must be in place for every sacrifice?

_____

2. What causes unanswered prayers?

_____

3. How can someone be found guilty of sending up strange fire before God today?

4. What does Proverbs 4:23 tells us about the heart?

_____

5. Name 3 blockades to answered prayer requests?

_____

6. What can you do to remove these blockades?

_____

7. Sin causes _____ and if this _____ is

unchecked it can lead to eternal _____ or death.

8. Only those who have _____ hands and a _____ heart may enter God's presence.

CHAPTER NINE
Tactics of Satan

Scripture makes it clear that Satan is a created being with limitations. Unlike God, he is not omnipresent and cannot be in multiple places at the same time. Because of this limitation, he employs a variety of tactics, strategies, and spiritual agendas to oppose, hinder, and intimidate the people of God. The Bible exhorts believers not to be ignorant of the enemy's devices (2 Corinthians 2:11). Understanding how Satan operates equips believers to stand firm, resist him effectively, and walk in victory.

Below are several of the primary tactics Satan uses to stop, discourage, or stifle the believer, along with biblical definitions and scriptural references that expose his schemes.

---

1. Accusation

Definition: A charge of wrongdoing; the imputation of guilt or blame.

Satan is identified in Scripture as "the accuser of the brethren." His goal is to remind believers constantly of their past failures, sins, and weaknesses in order to produce shame, guilt, and spiritual paralysis.

"For the accuser of our brothers and sisters, who accuses them before our God day and night, has been hurled down."
— **Revelation 12:10 (NIV)**

This tactic is illustrated in the vision of Joshua the high priest, where Satan stood at his right hand to accuse him. However, God Himself rebuked Satan and defended Joshua.

"The LORD rebuke you, Satan! Is not this man a burning stick snatched from the fire?"
— **Zechariah 3:1–2 (NIV)**

Accusation seeks to undermine identity and confidence, but God's grace silences the voice of the accuser.

---

2. Deception

Definition: To mislead by false appearance or false statements; to delude.

Deception is one of Satan's earliest and most effective tools. In the Garden of Eden, he distorted God's Word, questioned God's intent, and ultimately led humanity into disobedience.

"The serpent deceived me, and I ate."
— **Genesis 3:13 (NIV)**

Satan often mixes partial truth with lies, creating confusion and doubt. Deception causes people to question what God has clearly spoken and to substitute personal reasoning for divine truth.

---

3. Intimidation

Definition: To make timid; to instill fear.

Satan frequently uses threats, fear, and psychological warfare to intimidate God's people. The Assyrian king Sennacherib attempted to intimidate King Hezekiah and the people of Judah by mocking their faith and exaggerating his power.

"On what are you basing this confidence of yours?"
— **2 Kings 18:19 (NIV)**

Intimidation attempts to magnify the enemy's strength while minimizing God's power. Fear, however, is not from God (2 Timothy 1:7).

4. Condemnation

Definition: An expression of strong disapproval; judgment intended to destroy hope.

Condemnation seeks to convince believers that they are unworthy of forgiveness or restoration. While conviction from the Holy Spirit leads to repentance, condemnation leads to despair and separation.

The false accusations and condemnation brought against Jesus during His trial demonstrate how Satan uses this tactic to manipulate systems and people.

"They all condemned Him as worthy of death."
— **Mark 14:64 (NIV)**

Romans 8:1 reminds believers that *"there is now no condemnation for those who are in Christ Jesus."*

---

5. Temptation

Definition: To entice or lure someone into sin or compromise.

Temptation is designed to appeal to human desire and weakness. Even Jesus was tempted by Satan, yet He overcame by standing firmly on the Word of God.

"Then Jesus was led by the Spirit into the wilderness to be tempted by the devil."
— **Matthew 4:1 (NIV)**

Each temptation Jesus faced was countered with Scripture, revealing that the Word of God is the believer's greatest defense against temptation.

---

6. Lying

Definition: A deliberate falsehood intended to deceive.

Jesus plainly identified Satan as the originator of lies.

"When he lies, he speaks his native language, for he is a liar and the father of lies."
— **John 8:44 (NIV)**

Lies distort reality, damage faith, and create false belief systems. Every lie must be confronted with truth from God's Word.

Conclusion

Satan's tactics—accusation, deception, intimidation, condemnation, temptation, and lying—are designed to weaken faith and disrupt a believer's walk with God.

However, none of these strategies are new, and none are greater than the authority believers have through Jesus Christ.

"Submit yourselves, then, to God. Resist the devil, and he will flee from you."
— **James 4:7 (NIV)**

When believers understand the enemy's methods and remain grounded in truth, they are empowered to stand confidently, overcome deception, and live victoriously in Christ.

Lesson Overview

Key Scriptures

John 8:44
Haggai 3:1, 2
Matthew 4:1-4
2 Kings 18:19-25
Genesis 3:1-5, 13
Revelation 12:10
Mark 14:60-65

Fill in the blank

1. Temptation to _____ or _____ todo something often regarded as _____, wrong, or immoral.

2. Accusation is a charge of _____;imputation of _____ or _____.

3. Lying is a _____ statement made with_____ intent to _____; an _____ untruth; a falsehood.

4. Deception: to _____ by a false appearance or _____; delude.

5. Condemnation is to _____ an unfavorable or _____ judgment on; indicate _____ disapproval of; censure.

6. Intimidation to make _____; fill with _____.

Matching

    Accusation   a. John 8:44

    Temptation   b. Matthew 4:1-4

    Intimidation   c. Revelation 12:2

    Deception   d. 2 Kings 18:19-25

    Condemnation e. Genesis 3:1-5, 12,13

    .Lying   f. Mark 14:60-65

CHAPTER TEN
What's in a Name?

When you hear the names **Jezebel** and **Elijah**, what immediately comes to mind? What about **Saul** and **Paul**? Names carry weight. They speak to identity, authority, character, and destiny. Throughout Scripture, names are not merely labels; they reveal purpose, assignment, and spiritual reality.

When God first revealed Himself to the children of Israel, He did so through His **names**—each one unveiling a distinct attribute of His nature. Through these names, God taught His people how to relate to Him, how to trust Him, and how to approach Him according to their specific needs. In essence, God introduced covenant relationship by revealing who He is.

By identifying God's revealed name and matching it to their situation, the Israelites learned how to engage His power and presence.

The Revealed Names of God

- **El Elyon** — *God Most High* (Genesis 14:18)
- **El Olam** — *The Everlasting God* (Genesis 21:33)

- **El Shaddai** — *Almighty God* (Genesis 17:1)
- **YHWH** — *I AM, the All-Sufficient One* (Exodus 3:14)
- **Jehovah Nissi** — *The Lord My Banner* (Exodus 17:15)
- **Jehovah Rapha** — *The Lord Who Heals* (Exodus 15:26)
- **Jehovah Sabaoth** — *The Lord of Hosts* (1 Samuel 1:3, 11)
- **Jehovah Shalom** — *The Lord Is Peace* (Judges 6:24)
- **Jehovah Shammah** — *The Lord Is There* (Ezekiel 48:35; Exodus 33:14–15)
- **Jehovah Tsidkenu** — *The Lord Our Righteousness* (Jeremiah 23:6)
- **Jehovah Jireh** — *The Lord Will Provide* (Genesis 22:13–14)

Each name revealed not only who God is, but how He functions on behalf of His people.

Preparing the Way for a New Covenant

Although the old covenant revealed God's power and holiness, it was limited by human weakness and external obedience. God, in His wisdom and mercy, began preparing humanity for a **new covenant**—one that would move beyond external rituals and transform the human heart.

Through the prophet Jeremiah, God declared:

"The days are coming... when I will make a new covenant... I will put my law in their minds and write it on their hearts. I will be their God, and they will be my people... For I will forgive their wickedness and will remember their sins no more."
— **Jeremiah 31:31–34 (NIV)**

This new covenant would no longer rely on sacrifices offered through priests alone, but on an intimate, personal relationship between God and His people.

The Name Above Every Name

To fully introduce this new covenant, God revealed Himself in an entirely new way—not through a title, but through a **Person**. In the New Testament, God revealed Himself through His only begotten Son, **Jesus Christ**.

Jesus became the living expression of every name and attribute God had ever revealed. Through His life, death, and resurrection, His name took on authority, power, and access never before granted to humanity.

When Jesus willingly offered Himself as the ultimate sacrifice, His name became the divine authorization—the **signet ring of heaven**—that validates every prayer and petition brought before God.

"And I will do whatever you ask in My name, so that the Father may be glorified in the Son."
— **John 14:13 (NIV)**

Praying in the name of Jesus is not a ritual closing statement; it is an invocation of authority rooted in covenant relationship.

The Power of His Name

Jesus explained to His disciples that His death would usher in a new spiritual order. No longer would people need a human intermediary to approach God. Through Christ, every believer would have direct access to the Father.

Under the old system, worshipers had to bring sacrifices to the temple and rely on the high priest to intercede on their behalf. Jesus' death removed that barrier. He became both the sacrifice and the mediator.

Because Jesus humbled Himself—enduring the cross, shame, and death—God exalted Him and bestowed upon Him unparalleled authority.

"Therefore God exalted Him to the highest place and gave Him the name that is above every name, that at the name of Jesus every knee should bow... and every tongue confess that Jesus Christ is Lord."
— **Philippians 2:9–11 (NIV)**

His name commands heaven, earth, and the realm beneath. It carries redemptive power, covenant authority, and divine endorsement.

Conclusion

What's in a name? Everything.

The names of God reveal His nature. The name of Jesus releases His authority.

When believers pray in the name of Jesus—according to His will—they are not making empty requests. They are standing on covenant ground, backed by the authority of heaven, and engaging the full power of God made available through Christ.

Lesson Overview

Key Scriptures

Matthew 16:13-18
Acts 10:38
Ephesians 1:17-23
John 1:29
John 14:21
Revelation 19:16
John 10:7
Genesis 14:18
Genesis 21:33
Genesis 17:1
Exodus 3:14
Exodus 17:15
Exodus 15:26
1 Samuel 1:3, 11
Judges 6:24
Ezekiel 48:35
Exodus 33:14, 15
Jeremiah 23:6
Genesis 22:13, 14

1. What does a name do?
   _____

2. What did God do to introduce Himself to His people?
   _____

3. God does everything with what in mind?
   _____

4. The name of the Lord brings _____ for the righteous.5. Jesus' death birthed a new dispensation that will _____ the old religious structure.6. Name three of God's covenantal names?

   1. _____
   2. _____
   3. _____

7. What is the highest name mentioned in the Bible?

   _____

8. What does the name of Jesus cause the entire creation to do?

   _____

PRAYER 101

CONCLUSION

Throughout this manual, we have explored the vital role of prayer in the life of the believer. We examined the different types of prayer, biblical methodologies for praying effectively, and the spiritual hindrances that can obstruct our communication with God. Each chapter was designed to deepen understanding, sharpen discernment, and equip believers to approach prayer with confidence, clarity, and authority.

At its core, prayer is simply communication with God—speaking with Him and listening for His response. It is not a religious ritual, but a Spirit-led interaction that connects heaven and earth. Everything that manifests in the natural realm is first conceived in the spiritual realm, and prayer is the womb through which God's purposes are birthed into time and space. Nothing of eternal significance occurs apart from prayer.

For prayer to be effective, the believer must learn to steward both the **mind** and the **heart**. A disciplined thought life, a yielded spirit, and a growing sensitivity to the leading of the Holy Spirit are essential. Effective prayer is not accidental; it is intentional. It is developed through understanding, practiced with faith, and sustained through relationship with God.

As you move forward, allow prayer to become not merely an activity, but a lifestyle. Let it shape your decisions, guard your heart, and align your will with God's purposes. When prayer becomes central, power, clarity, and spiritual authority follow.

Knowledge Assessment

You are now encouraged to review and apply what you have learned. Attached is a **50-question assessment** compiled from the material covered throughout this manual. Take your time as you work through each question, answering thoughtfully and prayerfully. If you encounter a question you are unsure about, the corresponding chapter reference is provided at the end of each question to guide your review.

This assessment is not merely a test of knowledge, but an opportunity to reinforce understanding and strengthen your foundation in prayer.

Final Test

Matching

1. Lying   a. Haggai 3:1, 2
2. Temptation   b. Matthew 4:1-4
3. Intimidation   c. Mark 14:60-65
4. Deception   d. 2 Kings 18:19-25
5. Condemnation   e. Genesis 3:1-5, 13
6. Accusation   f. John 8:44

Chapter 9

7. Prayer is a vital _____ in the life of every believer; without prayer it is impossible for us to _____ with God. (Introduction)

8. Name 7 of the nine keys to executing prayer. (Ch. 6)

   1. _____

   2. _____

   3. _____

   4. _____

   5. _____

   6. _____

   7. _____

9. Praying anything _____ the accuracy of your prayers and causes you to both _____ hit and _____ miss your _____ target. (Ch.2)

10. What is prayer? (Introduction)

_____

11. T or F _____ There is only one type of prayer. (Ch. 5)

12. The enemy attacks our relationship with God by attempting to _____ our communication. (Ch. 8)

13. Name 3 blockades to answered prayer requests? (Ch. 8)

14. Lying is a _____ statement made with _____ intent to _____; an _____ untruth; a falsehood. (Ch. 9)

15. Examples of power displayed in prayer (Introduction)
- Jesus
- Elijah
- Peter
- Paul

16. According to Genesis 1:26 what was man given?

(Introduction)
17. T or F _____ Only some men, or were created in God's image and given dominion over all things. (Introduction)

18. T or F _____ We should not expect God to bless us. (Ch. 6)

19. Nothing can enter this _____ unless man says or allows it. (Introduction)

Just as Elijah, James, Moses and John were _____ so are we, and we have _____ been given dominion. (Introduction)

(A.) ____ God only hears the leadership, and doesn't hear me. (Ch. 7) Jn 14:12-14 **(B.)** Jer. 33:2,3 **(C)** Luke 18:1-8 **(D)** None of the above

T or F ____ If man allows something to enter the earth he cannot subdue that force or bring it under governmental control. (Introduction)

23. What is the highest name mentioned in the Bible? (Ch. 10)

_____

24. T or F _____ Name 2 myths that people believe? (Ch. 8)

25. T or F _____ We are children of God, and heirs to His promises. (Ch. 6)

Accusation is a charge of _____; imputation of _____ or _____. (Ch. 9)

27. What are three dynamics of prayer? (Ch. 2)
   1. _____

   2. _____

   3. _____

28. How did God create the earth? (Ch. 4)
_____

29. Our reign and authority are not based off the title or position we _____, but the God we _____.(Introduction)

30. What is the formula involved with prayer? (Ch. 2)

_____

31. ____Agreement

32. ____Spiritual Warfare

33. ____Petition

34. ____Thanksgiving

35. ____Tongues

36. ____Supplication

37. ____Praise

38. ____Intercession

39. ____Confession

40. ____Worship

41. ____Faith

(A) A solemn supplication or request to a superior authority.

(B) Your expressed appreciation for what God has done for you.

(C) Avowal; admission; acknowledgement; a confession of incompetence; an admission of misdeeds or faults.

(D) Standing in the gap for another or stand in someone else's place.

(E) Expression of approval, commendation or admiration.

(F) To ask for humbly or earnestly, as by praying. To make humble entreaty to; beseech.

(G) Thanking or praising God for who He is, not what He can do.

(H) Spirit to spirit communication with God.

(I) Steadfast belief.

(J) Harmony of opinions, actions of characters.

(K) The art of warring in the realm of the spirit.

42. Praying anything _____ the accuracy of your prayers and causes you to both _____ and _____ your _____ target. (Ch. 2)

43. What causes unanswered prayers? (Ch. 8)

_____

44. What is focus? (Ch. 2)

_____

45. What is stance and why is it important? (Ch. 2)

_____

46. Jesus' death birthed a new dispensation that will _____ the old religious structure. (Ch. 10)

47. What is deception? (Ch. 9)

_____

48. The enemy attacks our relationship with God by attempting to _____ our communication. (Ch. 8)

49. One must _____ the privileges, promises and restrictions _____ in God's Word for themselves.(Ch. 6)

50. Name three of God's covenantal names? (Ch. 10)

   1. _____

   2. _____

2. _____

TAMIYA D. LEWIS

www.ingramcontent.com/pod-product-compliance
Lightning Source LLC
Chambersburg PA
CBHW070937080526
44589CB00013B/1539